Becoming a Learning Detective™

contents

Becoming a Learning Detective© is one in a series of Let Me Learn Skills Books© **r more information, please call 856-553-6281.**

Becoming a Learning Detective© s produced in cooperation with **A+ Media, Inc.**

Publisher
Julio Abreu

Editorial Director
Alan Lenhoff

Senior Art Director and Illustrator
Priscilla Jeschke

1. GETTING STARTED

Dear New Detective,

Welcome to the Let Me Learn Detective Society!

Did you know that your fingerprint is different from anyone else's in the entire world? Just like your fingerprint, the way you learn is unique to you, too. Our mission here is to help you find your own unique combination of learning strategies—to learn how *you* learn.

What Will I Be Learning?

"Why is it important to know how I learn?" you may ask. "Why take the time to do that?"

When you begin a task, do you *think*, "Why am I doing this?" Or, "This is so much fun, I can't wait to take this home to work on it!"

When you are working on an assignment, do you ever *feel* stressed that it is not working out the way you expected it to, or do you *feel* excited when you think about sharing the finished product with others when it's done?

And when you're finished with a project, do you ever decide not to *do* it that way again, or do you keep it as a model for how to *do* the next project?

The point is: Everyone *thinks*, *feels*, and *does* things differently based on how they learn. When you know *how* you learn, you can explain how you succeeded in an assignment. You can also change what didn't work if you did not succeed.

You can take control of your learning and be the most successful learner you can be!

Sherlock

p.s. Be sure to get your membership card. It's on the back cover.

What Will I Do in This Book?

The mission of the Let Me Learn Detective Society is to help you:

1. **DISCOVER** your unique "learning fingerprint" by understanding your learning connections.
2. **RECOGNIZE** how to use your learning connections to handle learning challenges.
3. **KNOW** how to use your learning connections in school, home, and other places.

Beginning the Case

Call it "The Case of the Confident Learner"—you! Your first task as a detective is to gather evidence about yourself as a learner.

Where do you learn best—at school, at home, or elsewhere? What do you like to do in order to learn something?

To organize your evidence, create a "triorama." Start with an 8" x 8" square sheet of blank paper. You will also need scissors, colored pencils, and glue.

1. **Fold the paper from the top left corner to the bottom right corner to make a triangle.**
2. **Fold over the triangle to make another, smaller triangle.**
3. **Open up the sheet, and cut one of the folded lines from the edge to the center.**
4. **On "A," draw a picture that answers this question:** Where do I learn best? (home, school, outdoors, etc.)
   On "B," draw a picture that answers this question: What do I like to do there? (read, study nature, practice playing a sport, etc.)
   On "C," draw a picture of a floor (any kind you'd like).
5. **Put glue on "D." Slide "C" over "D" to glue the two panels together.** (You can use some extra pieces of paper to make 3-D figures to stand on the floor.)

WHEN YOU ARE FINISHED, have a good look at your triorama. What evidence does it provide about where and how you learn best?

- On a separate sheet of paper, write two sentences describing what you have drawn on "A" and "B."
- Do your drawings give you more ideas? Write a sentence telling more about where and how you like to learn.

Congratulations! You're on your way to solving "The Case of the Confident Learner."

THIS BOOK INCLUDES MANY ACTIVITIES that will help you to "crack the code" of your learning. You will read, discuss, engage in projects, and work with other detectives (including your teachers) to help you become a Super Sleuth of Learning!

Learning to Be a GREAT Detective!

Sherlock, superstar sleuth, has solved many cases. He has used many different ways to solve them, depending on the case.

For example, he solved **The Case of the Missing Lunchbox** by carefully reconstructing a sequence of events. When a Doyle Elementary School student, Watson, discovered that his lunchbox was gone, Sherlock traced all of Watson's activities that day, in order. He finally figured out that the lunchbox was in the basketball bin in the school gym.

He solved **The Case of the Mysterious Note** by carefully observing the scrawled lettering on a torn sheet of paper. He looked at the handwriting, the words, and the kind of ink that was used. By doing this, he discovered that the note was a to-do list that had been dropped in the hallway by the the Doyle principal, Ms. Arthur.

Detectives have different ways of solving cases. As part of his training to become a successful detective, Sherlock completed a form that helped him see that there are different ways to approach and solve different cases. This knowledge has helped him throughout his illustrious career. It can help you to solve **The Case of the Confident Learner—You!** and become more confident as a learner, too.

Here is part of the form that Sherlock filled out to discover different ways of solving cases—and to understand better the different ways he learns.

Sherlock was asked to put one of these words or phrases in the place of each blank: *Never Ever, Almost Never, Sometimes, Almost Always, Always.* See how he filled in the form.

I <u>*always*</u> like to keep my desk neat.
I <u>*sometimes*</u> like to get clear directions before I begin any assignment.
I <u>*almost never*</u> like to build models of things I am working on.
I <u>*almost always*</u> like to write in my journal.
I <u>*almost always*</u> like to make up my own way of doing things.
I <u>*never ever*</u> am upset when directions are changed.

WHAT DO SHERLOCK'S ANSWERS tell us about the way he learns—and solves problems? How would YOU fill in the same form?

Sherlock became a top-notch gumshoe by learning something about himself. He discovered how he learns things, how he understands the information he receives about any case. He discovered that we don't all learn in the same way.

You too can be a better detective if you know how you learn most easily. In fact, your first case can be "The Secret of How I Learn."

Finding the Clues

To discover how you learn, you will need to think about yourself and fill out a form that describes how you do things. Have you ever done this kind of self-evaluation? It's easy and fun—if you remember that there are no "right" answers. There are only the answers that are right for YOU.

For example, let's say you were gathering clues to how you like to have a good time. You could fill out a form like this. Circle or underline the answer that fits you best.

1. **In my free time, I like to play sports.**
   Never Ever   Almost Never   Sometimes   Almost Always   Always
2. **In my free time, I like to read.**
   Never Ever   Almost Never   Sometimes   Almost Always   Always
3. **In my free time, I like to watch movies and videos.**
   Never Ever   Almost Never   Sometimes   Almost Always   Always
4. **In my free time, I like to build or create things.**
   Never Ever   Almost Never   Sometimes   Almost Always   Always
5. **In my free time, I like to hang out with my friends.**
   Never Ever   Almost Never   Sometimes   Almost Always   Always
6. **In my free time, I like to spend time with family members.**
   Never Ever   Almost Never   Sometimes   Almost Always   Always

How could a form like this tell you—and others who might read it—about how you prefer to spend your free time?

Can you write more statements about ways you like to spend your free time—statements that might help people who read them understand the things you like to do? ______________________________

____

____

You can use the same kind of form to discover how you learn—just as Sherlock did. Turn the page to do just that.

LEARNING CONNECTIONS INVENTORY

Name: ____

There are three parts to the Learning Connections Inventory.

- In **Part I** you are asked to respond to 28 different statements by selecting your answers from the five choices.
- In **Part II** you are asked for a written response to three questions.
- After completing Parts I and II, complete **Part III** to tally your responses.

Part I

This is a way to find out about how you accomplish learning tasks. There are 28 statements each followed by five phrases which read: *"never ever," "almost never," "sometimes," "almost always," and "always."*

Directions

Here is what you are to do.

1. **Read** each sentence carefully.
2. **Decide** how well it fits with how you learn.
3. **Mark an "X"** through the phrase that matches what you decided. Be sure that you X only one phrase for each statement.
4. **Complete** the three short answer questions to the best of your ability. Write as much or as little as you feel until you have answered the question accurately.

Let's Practice!

Sample Statements

A. I like to listen carefully when the teacher is giving directions.

never ever | almost never | some-times | almost always | always

B. I like to stand in the front of the class and act out skits or plays.

never ever | almost never | some-times | almost always | always

---

Words of Encouragement: Take the time you need and consider your response carefully. While there are no right or wrong answers, there are answers that are more accurate to who you are than others. Selecting answers from each category provides a more accurate picture of your specific learning processes.

Choosing answers is not always easy. Often, if you decide on your answer, you will select "sometimes" as a compromise. Rather than doing this, we encourage you to change the wording in a sentence or add to the wording so that you can select a response that is specific to you. Feel free to write any changes in the booklet. Most importantly, have fun, relax, and enjoy learning more about yourself.

1. I like to build and make things.

never ever | almost never | some-times | almost always | always

2. I need clear directions that tell me what to do before I begin my work.

never ever | almost never | some-times | almost always | always

3. I like to tell my teacher all about my very special ideas.

never ever | almost never | some-times | almost always | always

4. I like to memorize as much information as I can to show what I know.

never ever | almost never | some-times | almost always | always

5. I feel better when I take time to double check my answers.

never ever | almost never | some-times | almost always | always

6. I like to build things and explore new places.

never ever | almost never | some-times | almost always | always

7. I like knowing where to find the correct answer.

never ever | almost never | some-times | almost always | always

8. I like coming up with my own different ideas instead of doing things like everyone else.

never ever | almost never | some-times | almost always | always

9. I like showing what I know by taking tests and quizzes.

never ever | almost never | some-times | almost always | always

LEARNING CONNECTIONS INVENTORY

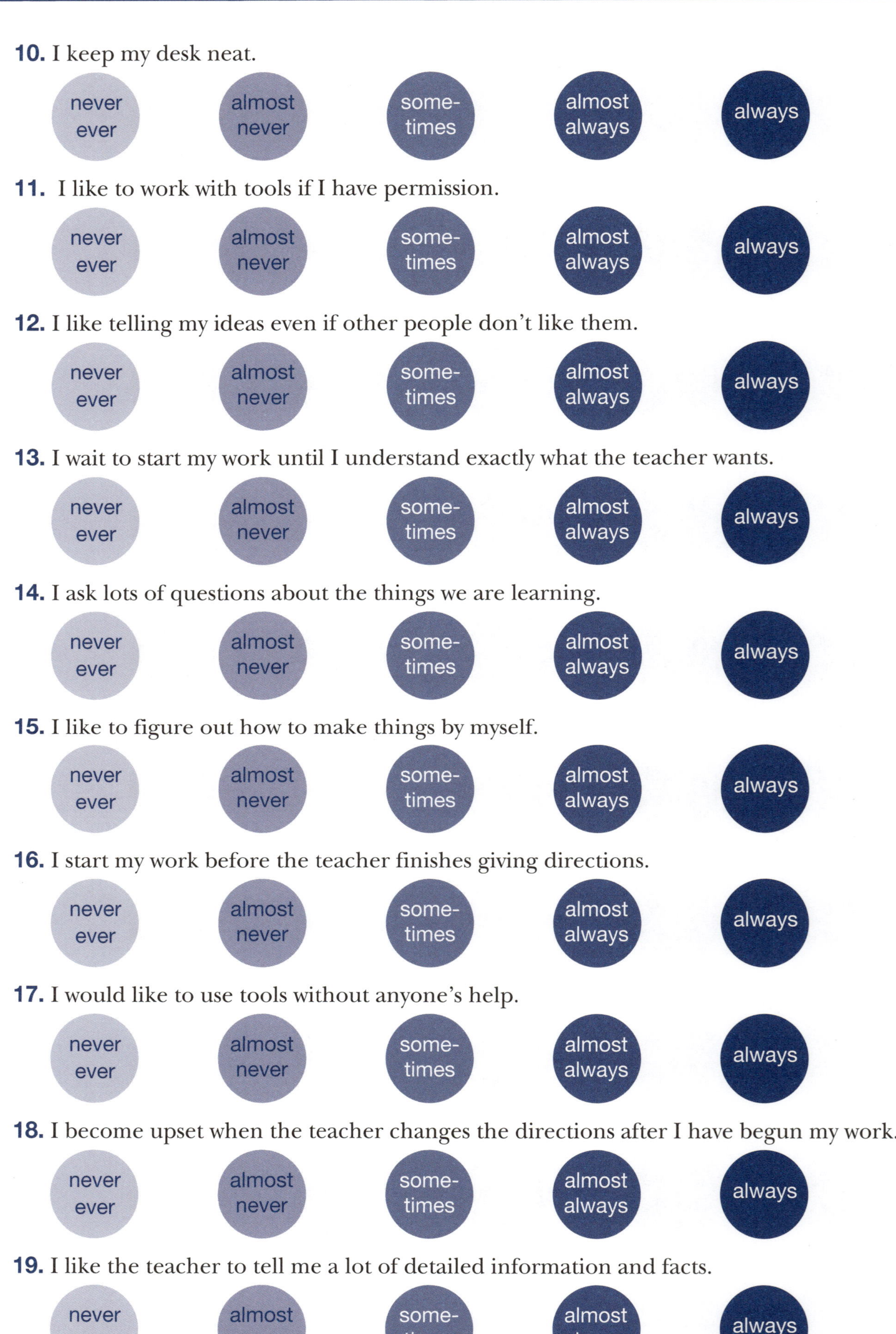

10. I keep my desk neat.

never ever | almost never | some-times | almost always | always

11. I like to work with tools if I have permission.

never ever | almost never | some-times | almost always | always

12. I like telling my ideas even if other people don't like them.

never ever | almost never | some-times | almost always | always

13. I wait to start my work until I understand exactly what the teacher wants.

never ever | almost never | some-times | almost always | always

14. I ask lots of questions about the things we are learning.

never ever | almost never | some-times | almost always | always

15. I like to figure out how to make things by myself.

never ever | almost never | some-times | almost always | always

16. I start my work before the teacher finishes giving directions.

never ever | almost never | some-times | almost always | always

17. I would like to use tools without anyone's help.

never ever | almost never | some-times | almost always | always

18. I become upset when the teacher changes the directions after I have begun my work.

never ever | almost never | some-times | almost always | always

19. I like the teacher to tell me a lot of detailed information and facts.

never ever | almost never | some-times | almost always | always

20. When my idea is better than the teacher, I want to use my idea.

never ever | almost never | some-times | almost always | always

21. I clean up my work area and put things back where they belong at home without being told to do so.

never ever | almost never | some-times | almost always | always

22. I like to take things apart and figure out how they work.

never ever | almost never | some-times | almost always | always

23. I call out my ideas before being called on.

never ever | almost never | some-times | almost always | always

24. I read a lot of books just for fun other than my school books.

never ever | almost never | some-times | almost always | always

25. I ask lots of questions because I enjoy knowing about many things.

never ever | almost never | some-times | almost always | always

26. I enjoy fixing things that don't work.

never ever | almost never | some-times | almost always | always

27. I am a very organized person.

never ever | almost never | some-times | almost always | always

28. I like to make up my own way of doing things.

never ever | almost never | some-times | almost always | always

Part II: Written Responses

Directions

Answer each of the following questions using the space provided. Write as much as you need until you feel you have answered the question completely.

1. Think of a difficult assignment. What made it hard or frustrating for you?

2. If you could choose, what would you do to show your teacher what you have learned?

3. What do you like to do for fun? How would you teach a friend to do it?

Part III: Scoring Sheet

Name: ______________________________

Directions

Score the responses for Questions 1-28 using **1** for "never ever," **2** for "almost never," **3** for "sometimes," **4** for "almost always," and **5** for "always." Next, transfer the score of each response to the center of the corresponding circle below. Add up the inserted numbers and record the total in the space at the end of each line. Transfer your total for each pattern to the bar graph at the bottom of the page.

PATTERNS								TOTAL
Sequential Learning	2 ○	5 ○	10 ○	13 ○	18 ○	21 ○	27 ○	______
Precise Learning	4 ○	7 ○	9 ○	14 ○	19 ○	24 ○	25 ○	______
Technical Learning	1 ○	6 ○	11 ○	15 ○	17 ○	22 ○	26 ○	______
Confluent Learning	3 ○	8 ○	12 ○	16 ○	20 ○	23 ○	28 ○	______

My Learning Connections

Graph the totals from each of the lines above on the appropriate bars below.

PATTERNS

	I avoid this pattern.	**I use this as needed.**	**I use this pattern first.**
	7 — 12 — 17	17 — 21 — 25	25 — 30 — 35
Sequential Learning			
Precise Learning			
Technical Learning			
Confluent Learning			

The Case of the Missing Mascot

Sherlock made his name as top detective at Doyle School by solving a baffling case.

What were the facts of the case?

The Doyle Elementary School mascot, the parrot Conan, disappeared two days before the big basketball game against arch-rival Wells School. Conan was found safe in a new birdcage on the roof of City Hall—but how had he gotten there?

Sherlock and other students at Doyle suspected that students from Wells had something to do with Conan's misadventures—but how could Sherlock prove it?

To solve the case:

Sherlock used precision: He collected parrot feathers that he found on the grounds outside Wells School.

He used sequence: He recreated the events surrounding Conan's disappearance—which included the fact that three Wells students were visiting Doyle that day. One of them, Wells Pep Club's president, Maurie Arity, excused herself for 15 minutes during lunch.

He used confluence: After the Doyle students found Conan atop City Hall, he noticed that Conan was saying a new phrase over and over again: "totally cool." He realized that this was one of Maurie Arity's favorite expressions….How could Conan have picked it up?

Sherlock felt that he almost had the case solved... but a key piece of evidence seemed to be missing. So he consulted with his friend Brianna, who sometimes liked to build things. She advised Sherlock to use **technical** learning by analyzing the wood and wire in Conan's birdcage. Sherlock discovered it was the kind used in the shop class at Wells. Eureka!

Sherlock solved the case, and the Wells students involved were punished. They had to dress up in parrot costumes and lead cheers for Doyle during the big game!

Sherlock cracked the case by using four learning patterns.

Like Sherlock, we all use these patterns to solve different learning challenges. Which pattern, or which set of patterns, we use, depends on what the learning situation calls for.

1. When we use the pattern of **PRECISION**, we deal with facts, and we ask lots of questions.
2. When we use the pattern of **SEQUENCE**, we organize information and do activities in steps.
3. When we use the **TECHNICAL** pattern, we solve problems by doing things, often with our hands.
4. When we use the **CONFLUENT** pattern, we understand things in our own, unique ways. We make new connections, and we take risks.

Pick the Pattern

Now it's your turn to investigate. Use the clues to figure out what learning patterns you think Sherlock's sidekick Brianna uses most comfortably. Circle the pattern letter that you think matches the clues. Put all of them together and figure out which pattern(s) she uses first, which she uses as needed, and which she avoids.

Clue #1: Brianna organizes all of her cases in color-coded file folders, and she always puts her work away when she is finished. **S P T C**

Clue #2: Brianna takes some notes when interviewing a potential culprit on the case. She usually lets Sherlock ask all of the questions. **S P T C**

Clue #3: Brianna enjoys using the tools from her detective spy kit (binoculars, tweezers, fingerprint lifting tape), but she does need help with the cases that require more mechanical tools (locks, screwdrivers, cameras). **S P T C**

Clue #4: Brianna is hesitant to jump in when working on a case, and she would rather use all of Sherlock's ideas than come up with one of her own. **S P T C**

Brianna's Learning Connections: ________________

Pattern Wise

The four ovals below are labeled with the words SEQUENCE, PRECISION, TECHNICAL, and CONFLUENCE. Of these four learning patterns, which do you think would best help you achieve each of the following challenges? Write the letter of each in the oval where you think it belongs.

Some are in-school challenges, while others are ones you might face out of school. There are no right and wrong answers. Also, some of the challenges might require the use of more than one learning pattern. Feel free to put some of the letters in more than one oval.

Use the lines below each challenge to explain why you put its letter in the oval(s) you did.

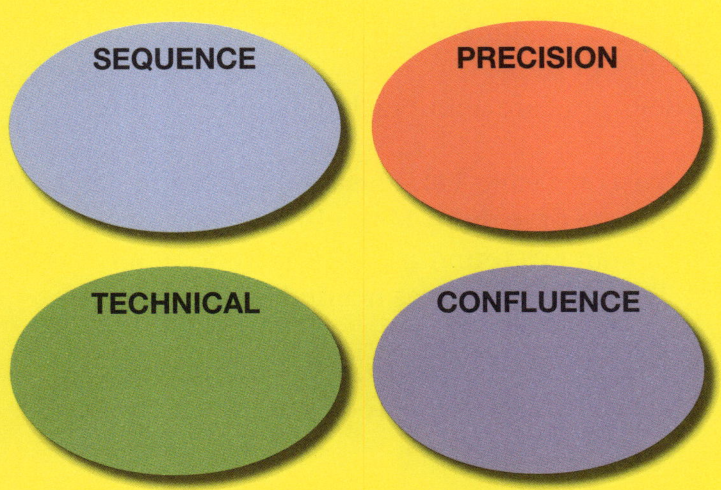

A. Explaining how magnets attract and repel ________

____

B. Writing a poem about a pet ________________

____

C. Acting out a scene from a favorite movie ________

____

D. Explaining the rules of a favorite sport for someone who knows nothing about it ________

____

E. Building a model of the solar system ________

____

F. Interviewing an adult relative about his or her childhood, and writing up the interview ________

____

G. Following directions to use a cell phone ________

____

H. Teaching yourself to play a video game that is new to you ________________

____

4. MY LEARNING FINGERPRINT

Solving "The Secret of How I Learn"

Congratulations! You've filled out the Learning Connections Inventory.

You've thought about how you learn, and you've given yourself some valuable clues to help you solve "The Secret of How I Learn." You now know more about how you use your **Sequential**, **Precise**, **Technical**, and **Confluent** Learning Patterns together.

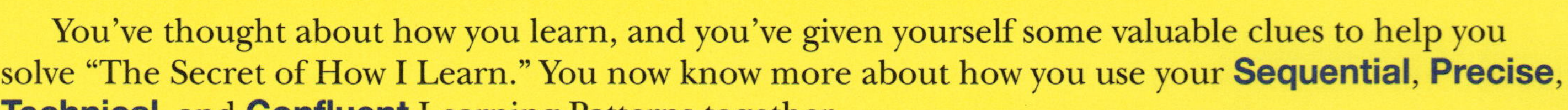

After Sherlock filled out the Learning Connections Inventory (LCI), here were his results as shown on the graph below:

Sequential: 20 **Technical:** 14
Precise: 31 **Confluent:** 32

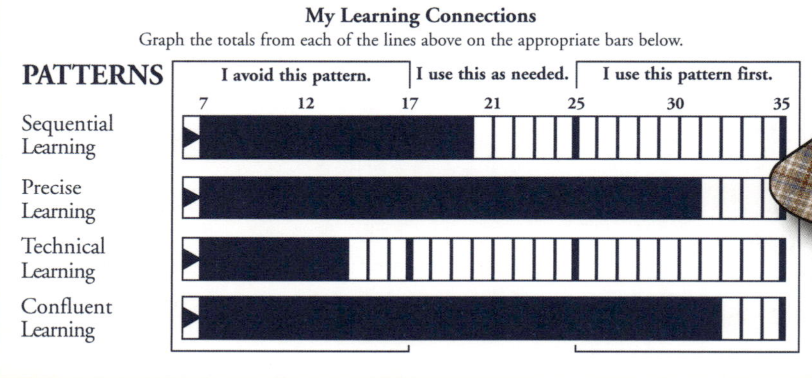

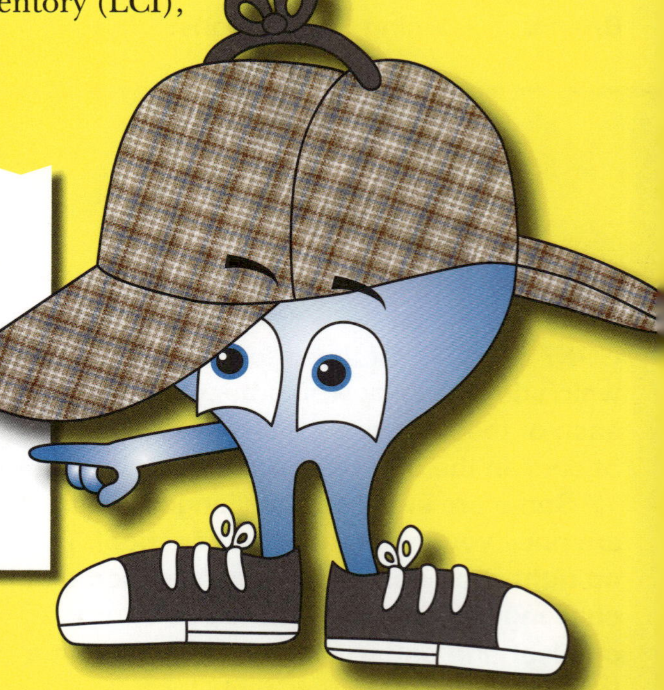

By filling out the LCI, here is what Sherlock found out about himself:

- **He uses the Precise and Confluent Learning Patterns *first*.** That means he deals with facts and asks a lot of questions (Precise Pattern) and understands things in his own way, makes new connections, and takes risks (Confluent Pattern).
- **He uses the Sequential Learning Pattern *as needed*.** That means that, when the situation calls for it, he organizes information and does activities in steps.
- **He *avoids* the Technical Learning Pattern.** He does not care about tackling a problem that requires him to work with his hands.

Do you remember how, in "The Case of the Missing Mascot" (page 14), Sherlock needed to get help from another detective to find clues that required the use of technical learning? It didn't occur to him to analyze the material used in the birdcage that Conan was found in. He had to be reminded to do this by his fellow detective, Brianna, who uses her Technical Pattern as needed. That's because Technical Learning is something that Sherlock avoided.

Thinking it over, Sherlock realized that, to be able to use all of the clues that he would find as a detective, he would have to learn how to recognize situations in which the Technical Pattern was needed, and develop strategies to use it.

Your Turn

1 **Do this activity only after completing the Learning Connections Inventory. If you haven't yet filled out the LCI, you can find it on pages 8-12. If you have completed the LCI, turn back to page 13 to see what your answers revealed about your learning fingerprint.**

Fill in the scores that you had for each of the four Learning Patterns:

Sequential ______ Precise ______ Technical ______ Confluent ______

- **Sequential Learning Pattern: Circle the statement that is true for you.**
  I avoid this pattern. I use this as needed. I use this pattern first.
- **Precise Learning Pattern: Circle the statement that is true for you.**
  I avoid this pattern. I use this as needed. I use this pattern first.
- **Technical Learning Pattern: Circle the statement that is true for you.**
  I avoid this pattern. I use this as needed. I use this pattern first.
- **Confluent Learning Pattern: Circle the statement that is true for you.**
  I avoid this pattern. I use this as needed. I use this pattern first.

2 **What do the results of your LCI tell about your Learning Fingerprint? Use each finger in the hand outline to draw a picture of something you have learned about using each Learning Pattern. On the thumb, write in your LCI results like this: S__ P__ T__ C__.**

How can you help yourself to use whatever learning pattern a situation calls for with comfort and confidence? Turn the page to learn about some techniques that have worked for other learners.

Using ALL My Learning Patterns

When he interpreted his Learning Connections Inventory, Sherlock discovered that he avoided using the Technical Learning Pattern.

Tether? ? ? Forge?

But he knew that some cases would require him to solve learning challenges that way. If he did not develop his Technical Reasoning, he would sometimes miss important clues.

For any of us, if we avoid any Learning Pattern, we need to **forge** (increase) its use. At the same time, if we tend to use any Learning Pattern first, we need to **tether** (control) its use, so we don't use it when it doesn't fit the learning challenge.

What, then, was Sherlock to do? He knew he needed to **forge** his use of technical reasoning. Sherlock's supervisor gave him some strategies:

To Forge Technical Learning:

- **Get in the habit** of showing others what he knows by demonstrating something or building it.
- **Use whatever tools are given** to him to show what he knows.
- **When presented with a challenge, look** for solutions that allow him to build or make something.

At the same time, Sherlock knew that he used his precise and confluent patterns first—sometimes turning to those patterns even if they weren't that useful for the case. His supervisor gave him a few strategies to **tether** his precise and confluent patterns:

To Tether Confluent Learning:

- **Limit the ideas** to 3 or fewer and choose just one.
- **Stick with one task** at a time.
- **Don't always jump in** without knowing what to do next.

To Tether Precise Learning:

- **Answer the immediate question**—add detail only if there is time.
- **Seek to prioritize the information**—to concentrate on what appears to be most important.
- **Remember that there are times** when he does not have to prove his point right away.

In other words, Sherlock would be a more versatile detective, one who uses all the clues available to him, if he learned to control two things: his desire to use his precise and confluent patterns, and his other desire to avoid using technical reasoning. He would be more successful if he could intentionally use whatever kind of reasoning the case called for.